BOOK OF QUESTIONS
FOR TEENS

BOOK OF QUESTIONS FOR TEENS

LADONNA HARRIS

authorHOUSE®

AuthorHouse™
1663 Liberty Drive
Bloomington, IN 47403
www.authorhouse.com
Phone: 1-800-839-8640

Published by AuthorHouse   07/26/2012

ISBN: 978-1-4772-4804-1 (sc)
ISBN: 978-1-4772-4809-6 (e)

ACKNOWLEDGEMENT

First given honor and praises to God for inspiring me to write this book, in which at times I thought was too silly to write. I truly thank God for reminding me to complete this project.

I would also like to thank my psychology and sociology students who entered into my class wanting to know what is "The Question of the Day", going to be? This book could not have happened without my students allowing me to look into their world and to ask questions, while receiving honest answers. I thank the students for sharing and educating me about what it is like to be a teenager and the issues that they go through.

Last, but not least I thank my family for encouraging me to complete "The Book of Questions for Teenagers". My husband for his kind words of encouragement and my children who also shared information that sometimes I really didn't need to know.

May God bless all of you for helping to make "The Book of Questions for Teens" possible.

1. You are sick and tired of your older brother or sister going in your room taking stuff out. You have even attempted to hide your favorite snacks in your room, but your sibling has found your hiding places and taken your snacks. You complain to your mother and father, but they do not do anything about it. You have decided to take things into your hand. How will you get revenge?

2. Your 16-year-old son or daughter came home with a hang over after staying out all night until 4:30 am. This is not the first time your child has stayed out all night and the child was grounded for several weeks before. What punishment will you impose on your son/daughter?

3. Your best friend is going though emotional abuse as her boyfriend or girlfriend continues to talk about other females or males and how good they look. Your best friend is very naive. What will you do to help your best friend?

4. A person that you have liked for a while stated that they would go out with you on one condition, if you get a tongue ring. What would you do?

5. One of your siblings smokes and sells marijuana. You are a little short on cash and you know that you could get an easy 500.00 by calling crime stoppers if you snitch on him or her. What would you do?

6. While working at a popular restaurant, you noticed the manager is using old produce and reusing foods that have been partially eaten by other customer. Would you confront the manger or would you just ignore it, because you really need the job?

7. Have you ever been mad enough to want to kill somebody and if so for what reason?

8. A rumor is going around the school that you are actively engaged with several sex partners and that you have a sexually transmitted disease. Additionally, you found out it was your brother who was spreading the rumor, because he is mad at you. What would you do?

9. Have you ever regretted doing something from your past that you wish you could take back? If so, what was it?

10. You had a series of plastic surgery done on your face and body to make you look like a movie star. Since then you have married a dream come true. Your partner wants to have a baby, but in the back of your mind, you are thinking of the possibilities of the baby looking like the old you. What will you do?

11. For 150,000.00 would you be willing to get a tattoo of a person you do not like on your forearm, knowing that you will not be able to remove the tattoo?

12. Who are your two best friends in the entire wide world and why?

13. Have you ever been caught with a fake ID trying to get in a club and if so where did you get the fake ID?

14. You been going out with this person for the last six month. High school graduation comes and you have not heard from the person all summer. The person never calls or come by your house. However, this person tells everyone that you are still dating him or her; what will you do about this situation?

15. You are invited to dinner at a friend's house. While you were there you become very uncomfortable, because you noticed your friend telling his/her mother to shut-up and he/she is being very disrespectful to his/her parents. What would you do?

15. There is this person that you have been hoping that he/or she will ask you to the prom. However, the person asks your best friend to the prom. Your best friend is not aware that you wanted to go out with this person. Will you tell your friend how you feel or do you just let it go? What will you do?

16. Someone very close to you is in pain, paralyzed and will die within a month. They beg you to give them poison so that they can die. What would you do? Also what if it were your mother or father?

17. What are you most thankful in your life?

18. Have you ever wished you were never born and if so why?

19. What is the most memorable event that you had in your life?

20. You have been in a relationship with your girlfriend or boyfriend for over a year. You believe the relationship is going well. However, your partner wants to break up and has stated that he/she is in love with the same sex. What will you do and how does this make you feel?

21. You have just been given 3 million dollars under the condition you must spend all the money within 48 hours with the following guidelines. You can only buy American products; you can't donate the money or share the money with your family; you must purchase at least 7 items, and you cannot spend all your money on clothes and you can not invest the money at all. How will you spend the money?

22. You adopted a baby boy 7 years ago and since then you have had two additional children. The adopted child continues to fight the other two children. In addition, the adopted child has been aggressive towards you and other adults. You investigate the child's biological parents and found out the kid's father was a murder and his mother was a heroin addict. What will you do?

23. If you found out that a good friend has AIDS would you avoid them? What if it was your brother or sister?

24. For 300,000.00 would you be willing to never again see or talk to your best friend?

25. If you could change two things about your personality, what would you change and why?

26. You recently won a 50,000.00 make over and you are allowed to make two changes to yourself. What changes would you make and why?

27. You have been given the choice to keep 100,000.00 to do with as you please or donate the money to a local homeless shelter. What will you do?

28. A donation of your skin is requested to help a burn victim at your school. The skin will come from your abdomen and will leave a large scar. Would you be willing to donate your skin to help a burn victim?

29. What do you do to get someone's attention that you really like?

30. What are three qualities that you like about yourself?

31. How would you describe yourself and how would your friends describe you?

32. What is the most dangerous thing you have done?

33. What is the difference between love and lust?

34. How often do you use the word love?

35. Your Great Grandmother has smoked for years and is need of a lung or she will die soon. All the family members have been tested and found not compatible, with the exception of you? Knowing that you have a 60% chance to live; would you donate your lung to your great grandmother?

36. Your child was born 3 month premature and you must decide if the doctors should try to save the child's hearing or sight. You must make the decision. Which will you pick, hearing or sight and why?

37. You have been randomly selected to make two new driving laws. One law must is for teenagers and one law must is implemented for the elderly (65 and older). What are the new laws you would impose for the two age groups?

38. You have been involved in a terrible traffic accident along with two of your best friends. You have 60 seconds to get your friends out of the burning car, before it explodes. Which friend will you save? One of your friends is sitting in the back seat behind the passenger seat and the other person leg is caught under the passenger seat. The other friend is in the front seat and is unconscious with a serious head wound and the door is jammed shut. What would your plan of action be?

39. One of your friends steals clothes, music, and movies as an occupation to help his/her mother pay the rent. They offer to sell the stolen items to you. Another friend says the police are watching the person who is trying to sell you stolen (bootleg) items. What would you do?

40. Your best friend mother asked questions if your best friend is doing drugs. Your best friend mother is very concerned about your friend and is in tears, because she does not know what to do with her child, because he/she seems out of control. You know that your friend is experimenting with drugs and needs help, but should you tell his/her mother? What would you do?

41. The court system passed a new law stating the parents are responsible for the actions and misconduct of their children and that they must be held accountable for their children actions. The law states that the parent must serve prison time for their children actions, such as fighting in school and stealing. As a parent, how will you keep yourself from going to prison for your children's action?

42. If you have a best friend that is overweight and you knew that there was possible health risks involved in their eating habits and lack of exercise. Would you recommend that they start an exercise program and diet? Would you simply not get involved?

43. What do you value most in a relationship?

44. You are engaged to get married in two months. However, your partner was involved in a serious automobile accident. Your partner is now a paraplegic. Will you continue your plans to marry the person or cancel? What will you do?

45. How would you describe a good friend?

46. Do you think you are good friend?

47. When you are trying to impress a date or someone you really like, what would you wear and talk about to impress the person?

48. Do you have more friends or associates and what is the difference?

49. Can you be friends with an ex-boyfriend or girlfriend?

50. The local sperm/egg bank is low on supplies and you have the opportunity to capitalize on the market by selling your sperm/egg, $50.00 per egg/ounce. However, the organization is only willing to collect the deposit through physical contact. Would you do it and is this prostitution?

51. You have finally found the perfect person that you enjoy talking to and spending time with daily. The person is a dream comes true. Both you and the other person feel the same way about each other. However, there is one problem the person you have strong feelings for is your best friend's, girl/boyfriend. What will you do?

52. Which situation is worse, being raped or being murdered and why?

53. Are you willing to stand up for what you believe in, even if there is a chance you would not be liked by your closet friends or even possibly die?

54. Do you consider yourself as a follower or leader?

55. If you knew you had only 6 months to live what would you change in your life or do different?

56. A street person stops you and ask you for money for food. The person personal hygiene is in terrible condition and it appears that he/she may be intoxicated. What will you do and why?

57. You found your ex-boy/girlfriend and your present boy/girl friend holding a long discussion about you and what you done in the past. You listen to them as they talk behind a closed door. You hear them laughing and making jokes about you. How will you react to the situation?

58. A 1000.00 reward has been offered to the person who would provide information regarding the person who has been pulling down the fire alarms at school. You really need the money to purchase your prom attire and to graduation pictures etc. However, you do not won't to be considered a snitch and besides the person is a close friend of yours. What will you do?

59. Would you be willing to live one month as a homeless person in New York City during the month of January for 200,000, knowing that you will not be able to live, sleep or eat the current way you do now. You will have to live the life of a homeless person. What will you do?

60. Have you ever cheated in school before and what do you consider cheating?

61. Several good friends of yours are constantly making fun of a person at the school you attend, because they do not smell good. The person that has been made fun of has confided in you that his/her family electricity has been turned off and that his/her parents currently has no money or a job. Do you stick up for the person or join in with the jokes?

62. You made a fantastic culture dish for a sociology project that is due the next day for a final grade. While turning your back to get a container to put the food in, you notice your dog drooling in the food and eating it. It is now 2:00 am and your project is due at 8:30 am. If you do not bring in the dish, you will not get the credit for the course. Also, there are additional ingredients required that you do not have in your house and five hours to make the dish. What will you do?

63. What do you consider a perfect life?

64. When was the last time you cried and do you think it is okay for guys to cry?

65. Would you be willing to give up television and computer/laptop for 4 years to help feed 8 billion hungry people for 20 years?

66. How often do you lie and have you ever told a lie and wondered why did you tell the lie? So have you ever lied just to make conversation?

67. If you could determine the gender and occupation of your child, what would you pick?

68. Your parents have conveyed to you that they are willing to change 3 current rules in your house. What rules would you change?

69. Your two best friends are pressuring you to skip school to go to the beach. They have everything planned out and they are just wanting on you to say yes. You are trying to decide if you should stay in school, because you have a final chemistry exam. What would you do?

70. You sign yourself out of school early to go home because you have a serious headache. As you enter in the house you noticed your mother on the couch passionately kissing a man that is not your dad? What will you do?

71. For $500,000.00, would you be willing to never ever again see or talk to your best friend?

72. Do you have a friend that never has money and is always borrowing money from you? If so, what would you do to help this person not be a leach?

73. What can people learn about you by looking at your friends?

74. What kind of people do you like to hang out with and why?

75. Are you introverted or extraverted?

76. Do you consider oral sex, sex? Why or why not?

77. You have been with this boy/girl for a couple weeks, but it seems like forever. You think you are falling in love. What do you do?

78. You and your best friend play sports. Your friend smokes weed, but you do not. You have told him many times not to do it, but he will not listen. A random drug test comes up and your friend is picked. Do you try to help him out?

79. Who do you consider to be a role model in your life and why?

80. You have a critical disease and have only 3 days to live and find a matching donor. Both your mother and father are matching donors and you love them both very much. Your parents have left the decision in your hand to pick who will donate their organs. Keep in mind, there is a 0% chance of survival for the donor. Whom will you pick?

81. What is the worst punishment you have received from your parents and what did you do to get the punishment?

82. There is a rumor out that your best friend is in love with you and has come out the closet. While thinking about the rumor, you replay in your mind all the times that you hung out, party together and even spent the night over each other's house. Would you question this person or avoid him/her all together?

83. You have a chance to live forever and become a millionaire at the small price of having irreversible plastic surgery to make yourself ugly. What will you do?

84. Before making a phone call do you rehearse what you are going to say and do you try to change your voice to make it sound deeper/sexier/ or softer?

85. Your best friend confides in you that they have been in a long list of bad relationships one after another for the last couple of years and that they are just fed up and feels like maybe they should experiment for a while with the same sex to see if the relationship will be better. What advice would you give your best friend?

86. One of your friends try to set you up with a nice girl/boy friend, because they know you have been picking the wrong type of person that is bad for you. You notice that the person is nice and cute, but he/she is boring. Do you over look the boring and try to make the relationship work?

87. Which type of life would you prefer, peaceful, boring and predictable life or a spontaneous, energetic, emotional and chaos successful life?

88. You really like this guy/girl and you want to be with them, but they play mind games. So, how would you get them to get on your level and stop playing games?

89. Have you ever had a dream that you wish would come true? If so what was the dream about?

90. What is the weirdest dream you have ever had in your life time?

91. If you could ask God three questions, what would you ask Him?

92. Your wonderful baby boy or girl has so many medical problems. You have been fired from your job and your health insurance is no longer valid. If you do not get the medication for you baby, the baby will die? How will you continue to receive medication for your baby?

93. You have being trying to get a job for over a year and finally, you received a job at a fast food restaurant. All your friends have been coming by trying to get free food. You really need your job and you know if you get caught you won't be able to get that car you want, however, you don't won't to let your friends down. What will you do? Keep in mind, the manger is keeping a close eye on all new employees.

94. Would you be willing to kill a person for a million dollar?

95. You have a critical disease that has affected one of your major organs and the doctor has given you three days to live unless you can find an organ donor. Your parent's organ match buy you have to choose which will live and which will give you the organ, knowing that one person will die. You love both of your parents, but who will you choose?

96. Your parents sent you to a camp for the summer. While at camp, you meet a really nice person and you are excited about your parents meeting your new friend. Just as you get ready to introduce your parents to your new friend, your friend runs to your dad and give him a hug and calls him Dad. Your Dad looks really shock and tries to explain. What will you do?

97. You are in lust with a guy or girl. You constantly have thoughts of this person and ways to be with the person. However, there is one problem, the person that you are in love with is your step sister/brother and they live in your house. What would you do?

98. You have been married for seven years and have two wonderful children. Your wife was killed in a terrible traffic accident and now you have to endure the hardship of being a single parent. Additionally, you find out that your beloved oldest son is in need of a blood transfusion and as the father you found out that you are not a match. All different thoughts start to race through your mind. What would you do about the situation?

99. Are you afraid to die? Why or why not?

100. Do you consider abortion murder? Why or why not?

101. You are dating someone who you have strong feelings for. At work, you are given a phone number by a co-worker. The coworker is also dating someone and says they just want to be friends. You accept the number and call the co-worker and hangout with the person. In the meant time, your very jealous significant other finds out somehow and is furious. How do you justify calling the person? Do you think it is okay to exchange phone numbers while in a serious relationship?

102. You just left the best party in your life and as you are driving home, you became distracted with thoughts of the party and you run a red stop light crashing into another vehicle. You know that you have been drinking and that if you are caught the police are going to take your license. Also, the person in the other car was killed instantly and you will be tried for murder. No one was at the accident scene. Would you stay and face the consequences or would you commit a hit and run?

103. Your cousin has been in a relationship and has gotten pregnant. Everybody is outrage about her getting pregnant and has demanded that she get abortion, because she is mentally challenged and so is the person she got pregnant by. Your cousin has come to you for advice. What will you tell her?

104. You and your best friend went to Cancun for spring break and you noticed that your friend is very drunk and doing things such as taking their clothes off that he/she might regret in the morning. You try to convince your friend to go back to the hotel with you, but the friend insisted that they could take care of themselves. Will you leave your friend or make him/her, leave with you?

105. One of your parents sits you down to have a serious talk with you about some issues that they have been going through. The parent stated that they have felt for a very long time, something was wrong with them; that he/she has been trapped in a wrong body and is going to have a sex change. What would your response be to the parent?

106. If you could be a famous person who would you pick and why?

107. You have been granted one supper athletic ability. What athletic ability would you choose and why?

108. You went to a good friend's house to eat dinner. While eating dinner you noticed that the silverware and dishes are dirty. Do you inform your friend about the dirty dishes or do you ignore the whole thing?

109. You are ship wrecked on a stranded island and you have only have enough time to save the food aboard the ship or your intimate partner (your intimate partner is unconscious, but breathing) before the ship sinks into the ocean. You have to choose between food and your intimate partner? What would you choose?

110. You have won, "be the president for a week". During that week, you will be able to make or change a law. What law will change or make?

111. What commercial on television do you think is offensive and promotes violence and sex?

112. Your parents have placed you on punishment due to your poor grades in school. The punishment they have imposed is no phone calls for two weeks and you can only have three outfits for the next two weeks. What outfits will you pick to wear the next two weeks?

113. What adjective and color best describes you?

114. You have a full ride scholarship to the college of your dreams. However, 3 months later you find out that your girlfriend or you are pregnant. A child is not in the equation of college. What will you do?

115. There have been several fires in your school bathroom and you know the identity of the person who has been setting the fires, because he/she is a good friend of your. However, the principle has accused an innocent person. The person will go to juvenile detention for two years. What will you do? Will you snitch on your friend to help out an innocent person?

116. When you go out to the malls or clubs do you change your name?

117. Have you ever dated two people at the same time and why?

118. Would you go out with a person with bad breath even though they look really sexy?

119. You have a friend that wears too much make up and really look stupid and behind her back people are always talking about her. However, in her face they tell her how good her make-up looks on her. Would you be honest and tell your friend the truth?

120. You have always played basketball, but you are a little apprehensive, because the whole team is homosexual and you are heterosexual. Also it is a know fact that if you want to play on the team you have to covert to homosexual. Also, this is your last year to get a scholarship. What will you do?

121. A lot of your team mates are using steroids to perform better. Everybody is faster and stronger than you, no matter how long you work out. Will you take steroids to increase your speed?

122. There is a rumor going around about your best friend that she had sex with several guys. You tell your friend about the rumor, because you know that your friend is a virgin and would not have sex unless she told you about it. Your friend confirms what you already knew that she is still a virgin. However, she has also informed you that she only had anal sex with those guys and that anal sex is not really sex. Would you agree or disagree with her and why?

123. Your parents are away for the weekend and have instructed you not to have anybody at the house. However, several of your friends would like to have a little got together. What would you do?

124. You dad gave you permission to use his brand new truck to use for work purpose only. However, your best friend called and said that they were stranded and needed a ride home. Being the good friend that you are you take the friend home. Although while backing up from your friend house you accidentally backed the truck into a brick mailbox and damaged the rear of the truck. Knowing that you are in serious trouble (grounded, drivers license taken away, etc). what will you tell your dad? Will you be honest or make up a lie?

125. Would you be willing to eat 300 live worms for 300,000?

126. As you enter into a local convince store you noticed that the store is being robbed. The robber is not aware that you have entered the store. What would you do?

127. When was the last time you lied to your parents and what was it about?

128. Your best friend had plans to go to the mall and movies. However, your best friend decides that he/she would rather hang out with their boy/girl friend. Would this bother you and if so why?

129. Would you be willing to run around your school during school hours naked, while singing a song very loud for 1 million dollars?

130. Is it okay for your best friend to go out with your ex-boyfriend or girlfriend?

131. Do you plan to marry for love or money?

132. What age do you stop spending the night at a friend house? In addition, when spending the night at a friend house do you sleep in the same bed or separate room?

133. Your 15-year-old daughter has a chance to make it big in the music industry. However, the music producer has stated that your daughter would sell more records if she poses almost nude in a video. What would you allow your daughter to do? What if it was your 15-year-old son?

134. Would you lie for a friend, knowing that if you get caught lying you could go to jail?

135. Would you be willing to die for a best friend?

136. Your best friend talks a lot of junk (smack, stuff) and is consistently getting into fights and you are always backing him/her up. However, you are tired of fighting for stupid reasons. What will you do or say to your friend?

137. What age will you talk to your daughter or son about sex?

138. Would you rather your parents, be parents or a friend?

139. You received an annonyoumus message on your answering machine, that your 11 year old daughter is actively having sex with numerous guys. What would you do? What if it was your son?

140. Your best friend stops by to get you to chill (hangout) with them in their new car. As you are driving around in the car, a police pulls the car over. Your friend all of a sudden tells you that the car is stolen and to be cool. Knowing that you may go to jail; would you tell on the person, so you wouldn't go to jail?

141. You noticed that your 13-year-old daughter has several cold sores around her mouth that never seems to go away. You are suspicious that she has a sexually transmitted disease. How will you handle this situation?

142. What would you do if you have a friend that is very nice, such as buying you lunch, paying your way into the movies and taking you where ever you want to go? However, the person is always complaining and talking down about your family. What would you do?

143. Your daughter or son has a new stereo and play station system. When you questioned them about the new equipment, they stated a friend gave it to them. However, several days later you find out that a local electronic store had been robbed. What will you do?

144. Would you pick your teenagers friends, knowing that some of their friends have criminal behavior and has been in trouble with the law?

145. You received a phone call from a concern parent, stating that your son or daughter is in a gang and has been seen selling drugs. What will you do?

146. Everybody that is somebody will be at this all night party. Your parents have already told you that you can't go. However, all your friends are pressuring you to go. What will you do? What if your boy/girlfriend tells you that if you don't go he/she will be with somebody else?

147. While out with your friend at a club you noticed him putting something in a girl's drink that he had been talking to all night. You really did not think much of what had happen that night, until your mother showed you a newspaper article of a girl that had been found half-dead and involved in a date rape. The picture is of the girl your friend had been talking to at the club. What would you do?

148. You have a friend that is suicidal and always talks about dying. Also, the person has given things away. What will you do?

149. You have a friend that loves making crank calls and at first you thought it was funny until the person called your house and left a message, stating that I'm having affair with your wife or husband. Your parents have been fighting and threatening divorce, since the phone call. Will you tell your parent that it was your friend that made the call?

150. Have you ever liked a but-er-head (you like everything except the person's face)?

151. Have you ever been jealous (how they look or what they have etc.) of a friend and why?

152. A person who you never met before asked you if you would take the SAT's for them, because they heard you are really smart. The person is willing to give you 200.00. What would you do?

153. Would you be willing to not change your clothes (you must wear the same clothes) for 60 days with the guarantee of 100,000.00 at the end of the 60 days?

154. Would you be willing to not comb your hair, brush your teeth or wash your face for 90 days with the assurance of world peace for 20 years?

155. Your little sister has been acting real strange lately. You finally get her to tell you what has been bothering her, but she has made you promise not to tell anyone. She tells you that she was molestested by a relative. What will you do?

156. You have been notified while at work that your son or daughter has been arrested for shoplifting. What will you do to your son or daughter?

157. Would you be willing to date your coach or teacher for money or an excellent letter grade?

158. What if any reactions would you have if another student approached you from your English class and told you that the teacher is failing you because of your race? What would you do and how would you go about proving what the person told you?

159. You are a very private person especially in your relationship. However, you have a friend that has never had sex and he/she wants you tell them about your relationship. What would you do?

160. What would you do if you were drafted into the military, knowing that you have a 75% chance of dying?

161. What would you consider the worst rumor a person could spread about you?

162. Would you tell a total stranger that they have something in their nose?

163. What would you do or say if you had a friend who was always scratching his/her private parts? Keep in mind there is a rumor that the person has an STD. Would you question the person about the itch?

164. For the 4th of July you were invited to go the lake with your best friend and parents. While at the lake you noticed the whole family smoking pot including the kids and they even offered you a joint. What will you do?

165. Your friend came to you crying and stated that she was pregnant, but her parents beat her so bad that she lost the baby. What will you do?

166. Your house is on fire and you are the only person who heard the fire alarm. The fire is spreading fast and you only have time to save one person other than yourself. You have a choice of saving your mother, father or a pet. Who will you save?

167. The doctors have told you that your unborn baby will not live due to an underdeveloped heart. You have a choice to have the baby or to have an abortion. What will you do?

168. You are in a hostile situation and you know for a fact that you will be tortured and killed even if you provide information. You are afraid you will disclose information that would cause others to be killed. Would you take your life to prevent others from dying?

169. You and your friend are camping in the middle of nowhere. Your best friend, who has just recently been diagnosed with AIDS, has just cut himself or herself badly while chopping firewood. You have no gloves and have open wounds all over your arms and hands from falling into a thorn bush earlier that day. What will you do? Your friend needs your assistance.

170. You and your friends went to a store with plans to steal abundance of clothes. Your friend told you to go in the store first to steal and that they will be waiting in the car. However, while you were in the store you were caught stealing. You were caught with over 1000.00 dollars of clothes, which is a misdemeanor. You have been informed by the police that they would possibly give you probation with a fine if you provide names of other people who steal. Also, they want to know the name of the person who drove you to the store. If you do not provide valid information, you will spend two years in a Juvenile detention. What will you do?

171. You and your boy/girl friend are deeply in love and you have just been told that his/her family is moving out of state in four weeks. Would you commit to a long distance relationship or would you break up with the person? What would you do?

172. You and your boy/girlfriend were in your car and you decided to let your boy/girlfriend drive your car. While driving your car they got into a major car accident, but it wasn't your boy/girlfriend's fault, but the insurance is in your name not your friend. Also, the car that hit you fled the scene before you could get information and you only have liability insurance on your Dad's car. What will you do?

173. What type of peer pressure is difficult to deal with and have you experience peer pressure?

174. What song would you dedicate to a love one (boy/girlfriend) and why?

175. What is your favorite song and why?

176. Would you continue to date your girlfriend if she played football on your high school team? In addition, would you continue to date your boyfriend if he joined ballet or cheerleading team?

177. Have you ever tried marijuana and other drugs and if so what drugs? Also, do you currently use drugs?

177. What is the perfect age to get married and why?

178. What event in history do you wish you could change and why?

179. Your race has changed and you must decide from the following ethnic group: African American, Native American or Hispanic. Which race will you choose and why?

180. You finally made it to a fortune 500 company. You are a Financial Executive and your salary is well in the six figures. Your dreams of succeeding in life have come true. You have the perfect life with the exception of your spouse who has a gambling problem. Your spouse gambling habit has gotten out of control and the debit is over his/ her head, so he/she wants you to provide top trade secrets to a loan shark. If you do not provide the information, your spouse will die and if you provide trade secret information then you will lose your job and possibly go to jail. What will you do?

The book is comprised of inviting and intriguing questions that result from secret information then you will loose your job and possibly peer pressure, morality, bizarre circumstances and everyday situations that teens go through.

I have used questions similar to these in the classroom as a psychology teacher and in-group and individual counseling sessions to generate thoughts, evaluate decision-making skills and to use as a guide to understanding teenager issues. I found the book to be very successful with helping students to talk about issues that they were experiencing.

My professional background includes working as an Adolescent and Child Psychologist, Career Counselor and for the last seven years, I have worked in the public school system as a Psychology Teacher and School Counselor, which afforded me the opportunity to become knowledgeable of the issues that teenagers go through. From the above experience, I have designed questions that teens find humorous, authentic, and informative. Although the title of the book reads for teenager, I am quite confident that teachers, counselors, and parents would benefit from the book as well.

Made in the USA
Las Vegas, NV
17 January 2024

84523444R00038